God
Is In
Your Pizza

For my boys...
May you always remember that Heaven is not some
place, it is inside of you always.

God is not some bearded man far off in the sky,

God's right here inside of you and in every pizza pie.

God is right there in your heart and in
your silly smile,

God is even with you when you wrestle crocodiles.

God is in the water and right there in the sand,

God is with you when you're happy and even when you're sad.

Be close to God by smiling, by breathing
deep and long...

You can even be with God while
singing your dog a song!

God's with you when you dance your dance, and
when you score a shot!

God's with you when you make mistakes,
and loves you a whole lot.

So when you help a stranger or give your friend a squeeze,

Remember God is in your heart and right
there in your cheese!

Made in the USA
Lexington, KY
07 May 2019